MW00950385

Lima

Travel Guide 2025

The Ultimate Companion for Discovering Landmarks, Dining, and Adventures"

Darby Z. Kranz

COPYRIGHT © 2024 BY DARBY Z. KRANZ

All rights reserved. No part of this publication may be reproduced, distributed, or transmitted in any form or by any means, including photocopying, recording, or other electronic or mechanical methods, without the prior written permission of the publisher, except in the case of brief quotations embodied in critical reviews and certain other noncommercial uses permitted by copyright law

Table of Contents

Chapter 1: Introduction

Overview of Lima

Lima, the capital city of Peru, is a vibrant metropolis that beautifully merges rich history with modern life. Nestled along the central coast of Peru, overlooking the Pacific Ocean, Lima is the country's largest city and serves as its political, cultural, and economic hub. Founded in 1535 by Spanish conquistador Francisco Pizarro, the city has a storied past that is reflected in its architecture, museums, and cultural institutions. The historical center of Lima was designated a UNESCO World Heritage Site in 1991 due to its stunning colonial buildings, plazas, and the remnants of pre-Columbian civilizations.

One of the striking features of Lima is its geographical diversity. The city is bordered by the Pacific Ocean to the west and the Andes mountains to the east, creating a unique landscape that includes sandy beaches, cliffs, and rolling hills. Lima enjoys a mild desert climate, characterized by cool, foggy winters and warm, sunny summers, making it an attractive destination year-round.

Culturally, Lima is a melting pot. It is home to a diverse population that reflects a blend of Indigenous, Spanish, African, and Asian heritages. This diversity is evident in the city's food, music, festivals, and customs. The culinary scene in Lima has gained international acclaim, with numerous restaurants ranked among the best in the world. The city is known as the gastronomic capital of

Latin America, famous for its fusion of traditional Peruvian ingredients with international flavors.

Lima also boasts a dynamic arts scene, with numerous galleries, theaters, and cultural events that showcase both local and international talent. The city hosts various festivals throughout the year, celebrating everything from gastronomy to literature, music, and the arts, drawing visitors from all corners of the globe.

In terms of attractions, Lima offers a myriad of options for travelers. The historic center features stunning colonial architecture, such as the Government Palace, the Cathedral of Lima, and the San Francisco Monastery. The coastal districts of Miraflores and Barranco are renowned for their picturesque parks, art galleries, and bustling nightlife, making them popular among both locals and visitors.

As a major transportation hub in South America, Lima is easily accessible, with Jorge Chávez International Airport serving as the primary gateway for international travelers. This accessibility, combined with the city's rich cultural offerings and welcoming atmosphere, makes Lima an essential stop for those exploring Peru and South America.

Significance of Lima as a Travel Destination

Lima's significance as a travel destination extends far beyond its historical and cultural attributes. As a city that embodies the essence of Peru, it serves as a starting point for many travelers embarking on journeys to explore the country's iconic sites, including Machu Picchu, the Amazon rainforest, and the Andes mountains. Lima is often referred to as the gateway to Peru, as it offers essential resources, services, and information for those venturing into the more remote areas of the country.

The culinary landscape of Lima is a significant draw for food enthusiasts and travelers seeking to experience authentic Peruvian cuisine. The city is home to an impressive number of top-rated restaurants, including Central, Maido, and Astrid y Gastón, which showcase the country's diverse flavors and innovative cooking techniques. Lima's unique positioning allows for a rich variety of ingredients, from fresh seafood sourced from the Pacific to diverse produce from the Andes, making it a haven for culinary exploration.

Additionally, Lima's status as a cultural center elevates its importance as a travel destination. The city is home to numerous museums, such as the Larco Museum, which houses an extensive collection of pre-Columbian art and artifacts, and the National Museum of Anthropology, Archaeology, and History, which offers insights into

Peru's ancient civilizations. These institutions provide travelers with a deeper understanding of the country's rich cultural heritage and history.

Lima also serves as a crucial location for cultural exchange. The city hosts various international events, festivals, and exhibitions that promote global dialogue and collaboration among artists, musicians, and thinkers. This cultural vibrancy attracts travelers looking for unique experiences and the opportunity to engage with the local community.

Moreover, Lima's accessibility and modern amenities make it a comfortable destination for travelers of all backgrounds. The city offers a range of accommodation options, from luxury hotels to budget-friendly hostels, catering to diverse preferences and budgets. The hospitality of the local people further enhances the travel experience, as many visitors find the city to be warm and welcoming.

Lima's significance as a travel destination lies in its rich history, culinary excellence, vibrant culture, and welcoming atmosphere. It serves as a gateway to the wonders of Peru while providing travelers with a unique and memorable experience. Whether you are exploring the ancient ruins, indulging in world-class cuisine, or immersing yourself in the local culture, Lima promises a captivating journey that will leave a lasting impression.

Chapter 2: Planning Your Trip

Choosing the Best Time to Visit

When planning a trip to Lima, one of the most important considerations is choosing the best time to visit. Lima enjoys a mild desert climate characterized by two main seasons: the dry season and the wet season. Understanding these seasonal variations will help you make the most of your experience in this vibrant city.

- Dry Season (May to October): The best time to visit Lima is during the dry season, which runs from May to October. During these months, the weather is relatively stable and dry, with cooler temperatures. Average daily temperatures range from 60°F (15°C) to 70°F (21°C). The sun often shines brightly, especially in the latter months of the season, providing an excellent opportunity to explore the city's outdoor attractions, such as parks, coastal cliffs, and beaches. Additionally, the dry season coincides with various cultural events and festivals in Lima, offering travelers a chance to experience the local culture.

- Wet Season (November to April): The wet season occurs from November to April, with January and February being the rainiest months. While Lima does receive some rainfall during this period, the weather remains mild, with average temperatures between 65°F (18°C) and 75°F (24°C). Although this season is less popular among tourists, visiting during these months can have its advantages. Fewer tourists mean less crowded attractions, and hotel prices may be lower. Additionally, the lush greenery that emerges after rainfall can make the city and surrounding areas particularly beautiful.

- Special Events and Festivals: When planning your trip, consider timing your visit to coincide with local festivals and events. For instance, the Feast of Corpus Christi in June and the Festival of Señor de los Milagros in October are significant cultural celebrations that draw large crowds. These events provide a unique insight into Lima's traditions and can enhance your travel experience.

Travel Insurance and Health Precautions

Before embarking on your journey to Lima, it's essential to consider travel insurance and health precautions to ensure a safe and enjoyable experience.

- Travel Insurance: Obtaining travel insurance is highly recommended for any trip, especially when traveling internationally. Travel insurance can provide coverage for unexpected events, such as trip cancellations, lost luggage, medical emergencies, and travel delays. When choosing a policy, consider the following:

- Coverage Options: Look for a plan that covers medical expenses, emergency evacuation, trip cancellations, and lost or stolen belongings. Ensure it includes coverage for COVID-19-related issues if necessary.

- Duration of Coverage: Make sure your insurance policy covers the entire duration of your stay in Lima.

- Provider Reputation: Select a reputable travel insurance provider known for excellent customer service and quick claims processing.

- Health Precautions: Lima is generally safe for tourists, but it is advisable to take specific health precautions. Here are some essential health tips:

- Vaccinations: Check with your healthcare provider to ensure you are up-to-date on routine vaccines. Consider vaccinations for hepatitis A, typhoid, and rabies, especially if you plan to venture outside the city.

- Food and Water Safety: To avoid foodborne illnesses, drink bottled water and eat at reputable restaurants. Avoid street food unless you are confident in its freshness and preparation.

- Altitude Sickness: While Lima itself is at a low altitude, if you plan to travel to higher elevations, such as Cusco or Machu Picchu, be aware of altitude sickness. Acclimatize gradually and consider medications to prevent symptoms.

- Mosquito Protection: Although Lima is not heavily affected by mosquito-borne diseases, it is wise to use insect repellent, especially if visiting areas with standing water.

Packing Tips for Lima's Climate

Packing for your trip to Lima requires some thought, as the city's climate can vary depending on the season and location. Here are some essential packing tips to ensure you are comfortable and prepared for your visit.

- Clothing: Given Lima's mild desert climate, layering is key. Pack light clothing made from breathable fabrics, such as cotton and linen, for daytime activities. In the cooler months, a light sweater or jacket is advisable for evenings and early mornings, as temperatures can drop. For those visiting during the wet season, consider packing a waterproof jacket or poncho, as well as an umbrella.

- Footwear: Comfortable walking shoes are a must for exploring the city's attractions and neighborhoods. If you plan on visiting the beach, bring flip-flops or sandals. If you intend to hike or visit the nearby mountains, pack sturdy hiking boots.

- Accessories: Don't forget essentials such as sunglasses, sunscreen, and a wide-brimmed hat for sun protection during outdoor activities. A reusable water bottle is also a great addition, helping you stay hydrated throughout your adventures.

- Cultural Considerations: While Lima is relatively cosmopolitan, modest clothing is recommended for visits to religious sites. Pack a scarf or shawl that can be used to cover your shoulders when necessary.

- Electronics: Lima uses the standard voltage of 220V, and the plug types are A and C. If your devices are not compatible, bring a travel adapter. Also, consider bringing a portable charger for your phone, as you may want to capture the stunning sights throughout the day.

By carefully considering the best time to visit, obtaining travel insurance, and packing appropriately for Lima's climate, you'll be well-prepared to enjoy this vibrant and culturally rich city. With its unique blend of history, gastronomy, and stunning landscapes, Lima promises an unforgettable travel experience.

Chapter 3: When to Visit

Seasonal Weather Patterns

Lima's climate is characterized by a mild desert coastal environment, with two distinct seasons: a dry, cooler winter (May to October) and a warm, more humid summer (November to April). These seasonal weather patterns have a significant impact on travel experiences, determining when activities like beach outings or city explorations are most enjoyable.

- Winter (May to October): During the winter months, Lima experiences cooler temperatures ranging from 60°F (15°C) to 70°F (21°C). The city is often covered in a dense, coastal fog known locally as *garúa*, which leads to overcast skies and damp conditions, especially in the morning and evening. Although it rarely rains in the traditional sense, the heavy mist can create a moist environment that makes everything feel a bit cooler. While Lima's winter might seem less inviting due to the cloudy weather, it is a great time for travelers who prefer cooler temperatures for walking tours and exploring the city's historical sites.

- Summer (November to April): Summer in Lima brings warmer temperatures, ranging between 75°F (24°C) and 85°F (29°C). This season is marked by sunny days and a more relaxed atmosphere, with locals flocking to the beaches along the city's coast. The combination of warm air and high humidity levels creates a perfect beach-going environment, making it an ideal time for visitors interested in water activities like surfing or simply soaking up the sun along the Costa Verde. Rain is rare in Lima during summer, but occasional drizzles can occur. This season's clear skies also make it a popular time for taking in the breathtaking views from Lima's coastal cliffs, such as those in the Miraflores district.

Overall, Lima's weather remains relatively stable compared to other cities in South America, with no extreme heat or cold. However, the choice of season can greatly influence the type of experience travelers have in the city, from beach days in summer to cooler urban explorations in winter.

Festivals and Events

Lima is a city rich in cultural celebrations and traditions, and timing your visit to coincide with a local festival can add a unique dimension to your trip. Festivals in Lima offer an opportunity to experience the city's vibrant culture through music, dance, religious rituals, and culinary delights.

- Feast of Corpus Christi (June): One of the most important religious celebrations in Lima, the Feast of Corpus Christi is celebrated in June. It includes elaborate processions through the city streets, featuring vibrant decorations, traditional music, and dances. The event is centered around the Cathedral of Lima and Plaza Mayor, where thousands of locals and tourists gather to witness the festivities. For travelers interested in experiencing Peru's deep-rooted Catholic traditions, this is an ideal time to visit.

- Festival of Señor de los Milagros (October): The Señor de los Milagros* or Lord of Miracles is another major religious celebration, taking place in October. It commemorates a 17th-century image of Christ that has survived multiple earthquakes. During the festival, a large religious icon is paraded through the streets of Lima, accompanied by thousands of devotees dressed in purple robes. The event is deeply moving and showcases the strong religious devotion of the local population.

- Mistura Food Festival (September): For food lovers, September is an excellent time to visit Lima, as it hosts the Mistura Food Festival, one of the largest culinary events in Latin America. This festival brings together top chefs and food vendors from all over Peru, offering a chance to sample the best of Peruvian cuisine in one place. Attendees can taste everything from classic dishes like *ceviche* and *anticuchos* to lesser-known regional specialties. Mistura is a celebration of Peru's rich culinary heritage, making it a must-visit for gastronomes.

Off-Peak vs. Peak Travel Seasons

When deciding when to visit Lima, it's helpful to consider the differences between the city's peak and off-peak travel seasons, as they affect everything from hotel prices to crowd levels.

- Peak Season (December to March): The peak season in Lima coincides with the city's summer months, when the weather is warmest and the skies are clear. This period includes the Christmas and New Year holidays, as well as local summer vacations. During these months, Lima's coastal areas, such as Miraflores and Barranco, are bustling with activity, as both locals and tourists take advantage of the beach-friendly weather. Hotels and restaurants can be fully booked, and prices for accommodations and tours tend to be higher due to increased demand. If you plan to visit during this period, it is advisable to make reservations well in advance to secure the best rates.

- Off-Peak Season (May to November): Lima's off-peak season corresponds with its winter months, characterized by cooler temperatures and overcast skies. This is an excellent time to visit for those looking to explore Lima's museums, historical landmarks, and cultural sites without the summer crowds. Additionally, hotel rates and airfare are generally lower during this time, making it a more budget-friendly option for travelers. Despite the cooler weather, the city's vibrant cultural life remains active, offering plenty of opportunities for sightseeing and enjoying local experiences.

- Shoulder Seasons: The months of April and November serve as transition periods between Lima's peak and off-peak seasons. These shoulder seasons can offer the best of both worlds, with fewer crowds and more pleasant weather. Temperatures during these months are mild, and the mist that characterizes the winter is less frequent. For those who prefer a balance of good weather and affordability, the shoulder seasons can be an ideal time to visit Lima.

The best time to visit Lima depends on your preferences for weather, crowd levels, and interest in local festivals. Whether you prefer the sun-soaked beaches of summer or the cooler cultural experiences of winter, Lima's diverse climate and vibrant events ensure that there is always something to enjoy, no matter when you visit.

Chapter 4: Budgeting for Your Trip

Average Daily Expenses

Understanding the average daily expenses in Lima can help you plan your trip more effectively, ensuring that you enjoy the city's rich cultural and culinary experiences without overspending. Depending on your travel style—whether you're a budget traveler, mid-range visitor, or luxury seeker—your expenses will vary. Here's a breakdown of what to expect.

Accommodation Costs:

- Budget Travelers: For those looking to save on accommodations, hostels and budget hotels are a great option. A dorm bed in a hostel can cost as little as $10-$20 per night, while private rooms in simple guesthouses or budget hotels can range from $25-$45 per night. Many budget accommodations are found in popular districts like Miraflores, which is safe and tourist-friendly.

- Mid-Range Travelers: If you prefer more comfort, mid-range hotels in areas like Miraflores and Barranco typically range from $60-$120 per night. These hotels often include breakfast and other amenities such as Wi-Fi.

- Luxury Travelers: For those seeking high-end comfort, Lima offers plenty of luxury hotels, especially in Miraflores and San Isidro districts. Expect to pay between $150 and $400+ per night for premium hotels like the JW Marriott or Belmond Miraflores Park.

Food and Drink:

- Budget Travelers: Eating in Lima can be very affordable if you stick to local eateries known as cevicherías and pollerías, or try the set lunch menus (*menú del día*) that many restaurants offer. A meal in a simple local restaurant can cost around $3-$7, and street food like anticuchos (grilled beef heart) or churros will set you back around $1-$2. A daily food budget of $10-$15 is manageable for budget travelers.

- Mid-Range Travelers: For mid-range options, dining in a sit-down restaurant can cost between $10 and $20 per person, with some higher-end options closer to $30 for a full meal. A mid-range daily food budget would be about $30-$50.

- Luxury Travelers: Lima's world-renowned fine dining scene is a must for food enthusiasts. High-end restaurants like Central or Maido will offer tasting menus that can range from $100-$200 per person, but these are experiences that are considered culinary highlights of South America. For a luxury dining experience, budget around $75-$150 per day.

Transportation Costs:

- Public Transport: Public transportation in Lima is very affordable, with bus fares typically costing less than $1 per ride. The city's Metropolitano bus system connects key areas, and the basic fare is about $0.60.

- Taxis and Ride-Sharing: Taxis are widely available, but it's recommended to use ride-sharing apps like Uber, Cabify, or Didi for safer and more transparent pricing. Short rides in the city range from $2 to $5, while a trip from the airport to Miraflores can cost around $10-$20. Daily transportation costs can range from $5-$10 if you use a mix of public transit and occasional rideshares.

Sightseeing and Activities:

- Most of Lima's cultural sites, including the historic center, parks, and coastal boardwalks, can be explored for free or for a small entrance fee. Entry fees to museums like the Larco Museum range from $5 to $10.

For guided tours of nearby archaeological sites like Pachacamac, expect to pay around $25-$40. A budget of $10-$20 per day should suffice for sightseeing.

Overall Daily Budget Estimates:

- Budget Travelers: $30-$50 per day
- Mid-Range Travelers: $60-$150 per day
- Luxury Travelers: $200+ per day

Currency Exchange Tips

Navigating currency exchange in Lima can help you save money and avoid unnecessary fees. The official currency of Peru is the Peruvian Sol (PEN). Here are some tips to make currency exchange easy and cost-effective.

Where to Exchange Currency:

- Banks and Exchange Houses (Casas de Cambio): Lima is home to many currency exchange offices, especially in tourist areas like Miraflores and San Isidro. These *casas de cambio* often offer competitive rates and are generally safe to use. Banks also provide exchange services, but they may have less favorable rates and longer wait times. Make sure to carry your passport when exchanging money at banks.

- Airports: Exchange rates at Jorge Chávez International Airport tend to be less favorable compared to those in the city center. If you need local currency immediately upon arrival, exchange a small amount at the airport for transportation and exchange larger amounts once you're in the city.
- ATMs: ATMs are widely available and allow you to withdraw cash directly in Peruvian Soles. Some ATMs charge a withdrawal fee of around $3-$5, so it's best to withdraw larger amounts to minimize these fees. Additionally, use ATMs that are inside banks or shopping centers for added security.

Avoiding Extra Fees:

- Credit and Debit Cards: Credit cards are widely accepted in mid-range and upscale establishments in Lima, but cash is often preferred for small purchases and in markets. Notify your bank about your travel plans to avoid having your card blocked for suspicious activity. Opt for cards that don't charge foreign transaction fees, as these can save you 2%-3% on each purchase.

- Always Ask for Prices in Soles: While some places in tourist areas may accept U.S. dollars, it's usually better to pay in soles to avoid poor exchange rates. Additionally, clarify prices in advance to avoid confusion.

Saving Money While Traveling in Lima

There are many ways to save money during your stay in Lima without compromising on the quality of your experience. Here are some practical tips for budget-conscious travelers.

Use Public Transport:

- Taking public buses, including the Metropolitano, is much cheaper than taxis or ride-sharing services. The Metropolitano system is efficient and connects many key parts of the city, including the historic center and Miraflores. If you plan to stay for several days, consider getting a rechargeable transport card for added convenience.

Eat Like a Local:

- Eating at local markets, street vendors, and small family-run eateries known as huariques is an excellent way to save on food costs while enjoying authentic Peruvian flavors. Many places offer *menú del día* (daily set menu) for lunch, which includes a starter, main dish, and a drink for around

$3-$5. This is a great way to experience local cuisine without breaking the bank.

Free and Low-Cost Attractions:

- Many of Lima's attractions, such as the scenic Malecón (boardwalk) in Miraflores, the bohemian streets of Barranco, and the historic plazas, are free to explore. Museums often have discounted or free admission days, usually on Sundays, making it an ideal time for budget travelers to visit. Check the websites of museums and cultural centers in advance to plan your visits.

Travel Off-Peak:

- Visiting Lima during the off-peak season (May to November) can help you save significantly on accommodations and flights. Hotels often offer discounts during these months, and attractions are less crowded, allowing you to enjoy a more relaxed experience.

Bargain and Shop at Local Markets:

- When shopping for souvenirs or handcrafted items at local markets, don't be afraid to haggle. Bargaining is common practice in Peru's markets, and a little negotiation can help you get better prices on unique items like alpaca textiles, ceramics, and jewelry.

By planning your budget carefully, you can enjoy all that Lima has to offer without overspending. With affordable food, accessible transport options, and a variety of free or low-cost attractions, Lima is a city that can be explored thoroughly on any budget.

Chapter 5: Essentials for Traveling

What to Pack

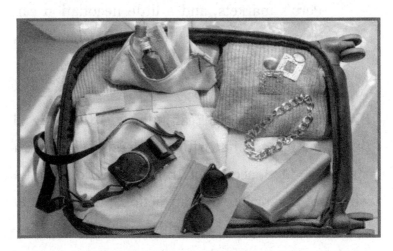

When packing for Lima, it's essential to consider the city's unique coastal desert climate and its range of activities, from exploring cultural sites to enjoying the beaches. Here's a guide to help you pack efficiently:

Clothing:

- Layered Clothing: Lima's weather can vary throughout the day, especially during the winter months (May to October) when mornings and evenings can be cool, but afternoons can warm up. Bring lightweight, breathable clothing for warmer days, such as t-shirts, blouses, and lightweight pants or skirts. Add layers like a light jacket or sweater for cooler evenings.
- Rain Gear (for Summer): While Lima doesn't experience heavy rain, the summer months (November to April) can be more humid, with occasional light drizzles. A lightweight, packable rain jacket or a small umbrella can come in handy.
- Comfortable Shoes: Lima is a city best explored on foot, especially in neighborhoods like Miraflores, Barranco, and the historic city center. Pack comfortable walking shoes or sneakers. If you plan to hike or explore sites like the ruins of

Pachacamac, consider bringing a sturdier pair of shoes or hiking boots.

- Beachwear: If you're visiting Lima during the summer or plan to spend time on the nearby beaches, bring a swimsuit, flip-flops, and a beach towel. Some beaches, like those along the Costa Verde, are popular spots for surfing, so pack accordingly if you plan to try out water sports.

Travel Essentials:

- Reusable Water Bottle: Staying hydrated is important, especially if you're walking around the city. A reusable water bottle is eco-friendly and allows you to keep water with you throughout the day.
- Sunscreen and Sunglasses: Even during the cooler months, Lima's UV index can be high, particularly in the coastal areas. A good sunscreen with a high SPF and a pair of sunglasses are essential to protect your skin and eyes from the sun.

- Travel Adapter: Peru uses a voltage of 220V, and the plug types are A and C (similar to European plugs). A travel adapter is necessary if your devices don't match these outlets. Many modern hotels and hostels in tourist areas may have dual-voltage outlets, but it's better to be prepared.

- Personal Medication and First Aid Kit: While pharmacies are widely available in Lima, it's wise to bring a small supply of personal medications and a basic first aid kit, especially if you plan to travel outside the city. Include items like band-aids, pain relievers, anti-diarrheal medication, and any prescription medications you may need.

Local Customs and Etiquette

Understanding Lima's local customs and social etiquette can help you make a good impression and ensure a respectful interaction with locals. Here are some key cultural insights:

Greetings:

- In Lima, greetings are typically friendly but somewhat formal. When meeting someone for the first time, a handshake is customary, especially in business settings. Among friends and acquaintances, a light kiss on the right cheek is common, even between men and women. It's polite to use the titles Señor (Mr.) or Señora (Mrs.) followed by the person's last name unless you're invited to use their first name.

- A simple greeting of "Buenos días" (Good morning), "Buenas tardes" (Good afternoon), or "Buenas noches" (Good evening) is appreciated in social settings and when entering shops or restaurants.

Respect for Local Traditions:

- Religion: Peru is a predominantly Catholic country, and religious traditions play a significant role in daily life. When visiting churches, such as the Cathedral of Lima or other religious sites, dress modestly by covering shoulders and avoiding shorts. It's also respectful to maintain a low voice inside churches and during religious ceremonies.

- Festivals: Peruvians celebrate many religious and cultural festivals, such as the *Señor de los Milagros* and the *Feast of Corpus Christi*. Participation or observation of these events should be done with respect for local customs and traditions.

Dining Etiquette:

When dining out, it is polite to wait for the host or person who invited you to indicate that it is time to begin eating. Additionally, leaving a small amount of food on your plate is often seen as a gesture that you were satisfied with the meal.

- Tipping: In restaurants, tipping is appreciated but not always expected. A tip of 10% is considered generous and is usually left in cash even if you pay with a credit card.

It is common to tip hotel staff, tour guides, and drivers for good service.

Personal Space and Communication:

- Peruvians tend to have a closer concept of personal space compared to many Western cultures. Standing close during conversations is normal, and stepping back may be considered rude. Making eye contact and showing attentiveness during conversations is important.
- Gift-Giving: If invited to a local's home, it's thoughtful to bring a small gift, such as chocolates or flowers, as a gesture of appreciation.

Safety Tips for Tourists

Lima is a bustling city with many tourist attractions, but like any major urban center, it's important to be mindful of safety. Here are some practical safety tips to ensure a worry-free trip:

Personal Belongings:

- Petty theft and pickpocketing can occur in crowded areas, such as markets, public transportation, and tourist hotspots like Miraflores and the historic center. To avoid this, use a crossbody bag with zippers and keep your belongings close to your body. Avoid displaying expensive jewelry, cameras, or electronics.

- When dining in outdoor cafes or restaurants, keep your bag on your lap or between your feet, rather than placing it on a chair or table.

Transportation Safety:

- While Lima's public transportation is affordable, it's best to use the Metropolitano bus system, as it is more regulated and safer than local buses. For taxis, using ride-sharing apps like Uber, Cabify, or Didi is recommended as they offer more secure and transparent pricing compared to hailing taxis on the street.

- When using ride-sharing services, verify the driver's details before getting into the car, and if possible, share your ride status with a friend or family member.

Areas to Be Cautious:

- While districts like Miraflores, San Isidro, and Barranco are generally safe for tourists, it's advisable to exercise caution in the historic center after dark and to avoid certain neighborhoods known for higher crime rates, such as Callao and some parts of downtown Lima.
- When exploring less-touristed areas or venturing into markets like Gamarra, go with a local guide or a trusted tour group.

Emergency Contacts:

- Save important phone numbers in your mobile device, including the local emergency services number (911), the contact information of your embassy or consulate, and the number of your hotel. It's also wise to carry a small card with the address of your accommodation, especially if language barriers arise.

Health and Hygiene:

- To avoid foodborne illnesses, drink bottled or filtered water, and be cautious with street food unless you are sure of its cleanliness. Washing your hands or using hand sanitizer before meals can help prevent stomach issues.
- Carrying a small amount of cash in various denominations is practical, but avoid carrying large sums of money or all of your credit cards in one place.

By keeping these packing guidelines, cultural insights, and safety tips in mind, you can ensure a smooth and enjoyable visit to Lima. Understanding local customs and taking simple precautions can greatly enhance your experience in this vibrant and diverse city.

Chapter 6: Entry and Visa Requirements

Visa Regulations for Different Nationalities

Lima, Peru, is a welcoming destination with relatively straightforward visa requirements for tourists. However, these requirements vary depending on the traveler's nationality, purpose of visit, and intended length of stay. Here's a detailed overview of what you need to know about visa regulations for visiting Lima:

Visa-Free Entry:

- Citizens from most countries in North America, Europe, and many parts of Latin America can enter Peru, including Lima, without needing a visa for short stays. This includes travelers from the United States, Canada, the United Kingdom, Australia, the

European Union, New Zealand, and several Asian countries like Japan and South Korea. Visa-free entry allows stays for up to 90 days, but the duration granted may vary depending on the immigration officer's decision upon entry. It's always best to verify with the Peruvian consulate or embassy in your home country before traveling to ensure there have been no changes to the policy.

- If you're entering without a visa, make sure your passport is valid for at least six months beyond your intended departure date from Peru. Additionally, you should have proof of onward travel, such as a return flight ticket, as immigration officers may request it.

Visa Requirements for Certain Nationalities:

- Travelers from countries in Africa, the Middle East, and some parts of Asia may need to obtain a tourist visa before arriving in Lima. This applies to citizens of countries like India, China, and Pakistan, among others. These tourists must apply for a visa at a Peruvian consulate or embassy in their home country or a neighboring country. It's recommended to apply at least one month before your planned departure date to allow time for processing.

- To apply for a tourist visa, you will typically need to submit a completed visa application form, a valid passport with at least six months of validity, passport-sized photos, proof of sufficient financial means (such as bank statements), and evidence of return or onward travel. Some consulates may also request a letter explaining the purpose of your visit and details of your planned itinerary in Peru.

Visa Extensions:

- Travelers who wish to stay in Peru longer than the initially granted period can apply for an extension. Extensions are generally available for up to 90 additional days, bringing the total possible stay to 180 days within a 12-month period. This process can be completed online through Peru's immigration website or at the Migraciones office in Lima. It's important to apply for an extension before your initial visa expires, as overstaying can result in fines or difficulty re-entering the country in the future.

Entry Procedures at Lima's Jorge Chávez International Airport

Jorge Chávez International Airport, located in Callao, serves as the main gateway to Lima and the rest of Peru. The airport is known for its efficient services and is well-equipped to handle the formalities of international arrivals. Here's a step-by-step overview of what to expect when arriving at Jorge Chávez International Airport:

Arrival and Immigration:

- Upon arrival, travelers will proceed to the immigration checkpoint, where you must present your passport and completed customs declaration form. The form is typically provided during your flight or can be found in the arrival hall of the airport. Make sure all required fields are filled out accurately, as incomplete forms can cause delays.

- During the immigration process, the officer may ask about the purpose of your visit, your travel itinerary, and how long you plan to stay. Be prepared to show a copy of your return or onward flight ticket. Travelers from visa-exempt countries will generally receive a tourist entry stamp in their passport, specifying the number of days they are permitted to stay. Always check that the entry stamp is properly marked with the correct number of days.

Customs Procedures:

- After clearing immigration, you will proceed to the baggage claim area to collect your luggage. Once you have your belongings, you will go through customs. In the customs area, you will hand over your completed customs declaration form to an officer. They may ask questions about the items you are bringing into the country, especially if you are carrying large amounts of cash, valuable goods, or items that need to be declared.

- Peru has regulations on certain goods, such as fresh produce, meats, and dairy products, which are prohibited from entering the country. It's important to familiarize yourself with these restrictions to avoid having items confiscated at the airport.

Security and Transportation:

- Jorge Chávez International Airport is well-known for its safety and security. However, like many large airports, it's important to keep an eye on your belongings, especially in crowded areas like the baggage claim. There are designated counters and kiosks for purchasing local SIM cards and arranging for taxi or shuttle services to your accommodation.

- Official airport taxis are the safest option for traveling from the airport to Lima's main districts like Miraflores or San Isidro. Always use the authorized taxi services found inside the airport terminal, as they offer fixed rates and a safer experience than unofficial drivers outside the airport.

Important Travel Documents to Carry

When traveling to Lima, it's crucial to carry certain documents to ensure a smooth entry into the country and to facilitate your stay. Here's a list of the essential travel documents to have on hand:

Passport:

- A valid passport is required for entry into Peru. It must be valid for at least six months beyond your planned departure date. It's a good idea to make a photocopy of your passport's information page and keep it separate from the original in case of loss or theft. Some travelers also store digital copies in a secure online location for easy access.

Visa (if applicable):
- If you need a tourist visa for entry into Peru, make sure to carry the original visa document and any supporting documents that were part of your visa application. It's also advisable to have a copy of the visa approval email or document, as this can be useful for clarification at immigration.

Proof of Onward Travel:
- Peruvian immigration officers may ask for proof that you plan to leave the country before the expiration of your permitted stay.

This is typically satisfied by showing a return airline ticket or an onward travel reservation. Having a printed copy of your flight details is recommended.

Travel Insurance Documents:

- Travel insurance is not required for entry into Peru, but it is highly recommended. A good travel insurance policy should cover medical emergencies, trip cancellations, lost baggage, and theft. Carry a copy of your travel insurance policy, including emergency contact numbers and details about coverage.

Vaccination Certificates (if applicable):

- While Peru does not require vaccinations for entry, travelers coming from certain countries in South America and sub-Saharan Africa may need to show proof of a yellow fever vaccination, especially if they plan to visit the Amazon region. It's advisable to have a yellow fever vaccination certificate if your travel plans include areas like Iquitos or Manu National Park.

Local Accommodation Information:

- Having a copy of your hotel reservation or accommodation details, including the address and phone number, can be helpful when filling out immigration forms and in case you need to provide proof of stay. It's also practical to have the information saved on your phone for easy access during your travels.

Emergency Contacts & Embassy Information:

- Keep a list of emergency contact numbers, including the contact information for your country's embassy or consulate in Lima. This can be invaluable in case of lost documents, legal issues, or other emergencies during your trip.

Carrying the right documents and understanding Lima's entry procedures can help ensure a smooth start to your visit. By being prepared and informed, you'll be able to focus on enjoying all the experiences that this vibrant city has to offer.

Chapter 7: Itinerary

Sample 5-Day Itinerary

Lima, the vibrant capital of Peru, offers a rich blend of historical landmarks, cultural experiences, and breathtaking coastal views. This 5-day itinerary is designed to give you a well-rounded experience of Lima's main attractions while allowing for both exploration and relaxation. Whether you're a history buff, a foodie, or someone seeking adventure, this plan ensures a fulfilling visit to this dynamic city.

Day 1: Discovering Lima's Historic Center
Morning:

- Plaza Mayor and Government Palace: Begin your journey at the heart of Lima's historic district—Plaza Mayor, also known as Plaza de Armas. This UNESCO World Heritage site is surrounded by key landmarks, including the Government Palace, which serves as the official residence of Peru's president. Arrive by 11:30 AM to catch the ceremonial Changing of the Guard in front of the palace, a colorful display of tradition.

- Cathedral of Lima: Located on the Plaza Mayor, the Cathedral of Lima is a stunning example of colonial architecture. Inside, you'll find the tomb of Francisco Pizarro, the Spanish conquistador who founded the city. Spend time admiring the intricate wood carvings and religious art.

Afternoon:

- Monastery of San Francisco: A short walk from Plaza Mayor, the Monastery of San Francisco is famous for its impressive library and catacombs, which served as a burial site in colonial times. A guided tour offers insights into Lima's colonial history and the architectural significance of this historic site.
- Lunch in a Traditional Restaurant: Enjoy lunch at a nearby local restaurant like *El

Cordano*, where you can sample traditional Peruvian dishes such as *lomo saltado* (stir-fried beef) or *ají de gallina* (creamy chicken stew).

Evening:

- Magic Water Circuit at Parque de la Reserva: End your first day with a visit to the Magic Water Circuit, a series of illuminated fountains set to music. It's an ideal way to unwind while enjoying the evening air. The park comes alive with light shows after sunset, providing a magical atmosphere perfect for a leisurely stroll.

Day 2: Coastal Views and Modern Lima
Morning:

- Miraflores Malecón: Start your day with a walk along the *Malecón* in Miraflores, a scenic path that stretches along Lima's cliffs overlooking the Pacific Ocean. Take in the stunning views and stop at *Parque del

Amor* (Love Park), known for its romantic mosaic benches and a large sculpture of a kissing couple.

- Paragliding Over the Pacific: For the adventurous, Miraflores is a great place to try paragliding. Soar over the coastline for an unforgettable view of Lima's beaches, cliffs, and cityscape. There are several reputable operators offering tandem flights.

Afternoon:

- Huaca Pucllana: Visit this ancient adobe and clay pyramid that dates back to pre-Inca times. The on-site museum provides fascinating insights into the history of the Lima culture that built this pyramid. Guided tours are available in English and Spanish.
- Lunch at a Seaside Restaurant: Head to *La Mar Cebichería*, one of Lima's most famous seafood restaurants, for a lunch featuring ceviche, Peru's national dish. Enjoy fresh

seafood prepared with local ingredients while taking in the coastal ambiance.

Evening:

- Larcomar Shopping Center: In the evening, explore Larcomar, a modern shopping complex built into the cliffs of Miraflores. It's a great spot for shopping, grabbing coffee, or enjoying dinner with a view. End your day with a cocktail at one of the bars overlooking the ocean.

Day 3: Art and Culture in Barranco

Morning:

- Exploring Barranco's Streets and Murals: Barranco, Lima's bohemian neighborhood, is known for its vibrant street art and colonial architecture. Spend the morning wandering through its charming streets, discovering murals and art galleries. Don't miss the *Puente de los Suspiros* (Bridge of Sighs), a popular spot for photos.

- Visit the Mario Testino Museum (MATE): This museum, dedicated to the work of the renowned Peruvian photographer Mario Testino, showcases stunning fashion photography and portraits. It's a must-see for art enthusiasts.

Afternoon:

- Lunch at a Barranco Café: Choose a cozy café like Isolina Taberna Peruana, known for its hearty traditional Peruvian dishes served in a welcoming atmosphere. Try the seco de res (braised beef stew) or *anticuchos* (grilled beef heart).
- Museo de Arte Contemporáneo (MAC): Visit the Museum of Contemporary Art to explore modern works by Peruvian and international artists. The museum's serene gardens and sleek architecture create a peaceful atmosphere for art lovers.

Evening:

- Live Music and Nightlife: Barranco is famous for its vibrant nightlife. Enjoy live music at one of the many bars or *peñas* (folk music venues). *La Noche de Barranco* is a popular spot for live bands and has a great atmosphere for an evening out.

Day 4: Day Trip to Pachacamac and Relaxation

Morning:

- Visit the Archaeological Site of Pachacamac: About an hour south of Lima, Pachacamac is an impressive ancient complex that dates back over a thousand years. Explore the temples, pyramids, and plazas that served as a major religious center in pre-Inca and Inca times. A guided tour provides valuable context about the site's significance.
- Beach Stop at Playa El Silencio: After your visit, stop at Playa El Silencio, a beautiful beach along the way back to Lima. Relax on the sand or take a dip in the Pacific Ocean.

Afternoon:

- Return to Lima for Lunch: Head back to the city and have lunch at *La Picantería*, a restaurant known for its traditional Peruvian cuisine served family-style. This is a great opportunity to try regional dishes from different parts of Peru.

Evening:

- Relaxing Evening in Miraflores: Unwind with a leisurely evening in Miraflores. Walk along Kennedy Park, known for its lively atmosphere and the friendly cats that roam around. If you're in the mood for a movie, visit the nearby cinemas or catch a performance at the *Teatro Británico*.

Day 5: Museums and Farewell to Lima
Morning:

- Museo Larco: Start your final day with a visit to Museo Larco, a must-see museum housed in an 18th-century vice-royal mansion. The museum is famous for its extensive collection of pre-Columbian artifacts, including ceramics, gold and silver pieces, and an impressive array of erotic pottery. The lush garden surrounding the museum offers a tranquil atmosphere.

- Lunch at the Museum's Café: Enjoy lunch at the museum's café, which offers a peaceful setting and a menu featuring Peruvian dishes with a modern twist.

Afternoon:

- Explore the Historic District of Pueblo Libre: Close to Museo Larco, Pueblo Libre is one of Lima's oldest neighborhoods. Visit the *Museo Nacional de Arqueología, Antropología e Historia del Perú*, which houses artifacts from different periods of Peru's history, including the Inca and pre-Inca civilizations.

Evening:

- Dinner in a Fine Dining Restaurant: For your final night in Lima, treat yourself to a memorable dining experience at *Central* or *Maido*, both of which are ranked among the world's best restaurants. Enjoy innovative dishes that highlight Peru's diverse culinary heritage.

- Sunset at the Malecón: End your trip with a sunset walk along the Malecón in Miraflores, taking in the stunning views over the Pacific Ocean. Reflect on your experiences and soak in the beauty of Lima before your departure.

This 5-day itinerary covers the best of Lima's historical sites, modern attractions, and local culture, ensuring that you make the most of your time in this fascinating city. With a balance of sightseeing, culinary adventures, and relaxation, this plan offers a comprehensive taste of what Lima has to offer.

Chapter 8: Hotels and Locations

Luxury Hotels

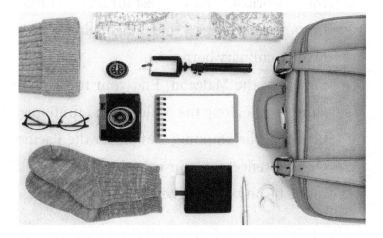

Lima, as Peru's capital and a major hub for business and tourism, is home to some of South America's most luxurious accommodations. Travelers seeking high-end experiences will find options that offer a blend of modern comforts, rich cultural heritage, and exceptional service. Here's a look at three of Lima's top luxury hotels, complete with detailed descriptions, pricing, and booking information.

1. Belmond Miraflores Park

- Location: Av. Malecón de la Reserva 1035, Miraflores, Lima
- Price: Starting at around $400 per night for a basic room, with rates rising to $1,200 or more for suites with ocean views and additional amenities.
- Booking Contact: +51 1 610 4000

Situated in the upscale district of Miraflores, the Belmond Miraflores Park offers an exclusive experience with breathtaking views of the Pacific Ocean. This hotel combines modern elegance with a taste of Peruvian culture, making it a top choice for both leisure and business travelers. The rooms are spacious and well-appointed, with floor-to-ceiling windows that allow guests to enjoy stunning sunsets over the ocean. Guests can unwind in the rooftop infinity pool, which provides panoramic views of the city and the sea.

The Belmond Miraflores Park also boasts a renowned restaurant, Tragaluz, where guests can savor contemporary Peruvian and international cuisine. For those seeking relaxation, the hotel's Zest Spa offers a range of treatments using natural Andean ingredients. Its prime location in Miraflores makes it easy for guests to explore nearby attractions, such as the Larcomar shopping center and the famous Miraflores boardwalk.

2. JW Marriott Hotel Lima

- Location: Malecón de la Reserva 615, Miraflores, Lima
- Price: Rates start at approximately $300 per night for a deluxe room and can go up to $900 or more for ocean-view suites.
- Booking Contact: +51 1 217 7000

Overlooking the scenic cliffs of Miraflores, the JW Marriott Hotel Lima is another top-tier choice for luxury travelers. The hotel's striking glass façade offers uninterrupted views of the Pacific Ocean, and many rooms come with floor-to-ceiling windows that maximize the stunning coastal scenery. The JW Marriott is known for its excellent service and attention to detail, ensuring a comfortable and personalized stay for its guests.

The hotel's amenities include a full-service spa, a heated outdoor pool, and a state-of-the-art fitness center. The culinary offerings are also a highlight, with La Vista Restaurant serving Peruvian and international dishes made from fresh, locally sourced ingredients. The JW Marriott's central location in Miraflores provides easy access to local attractions, such as the Miraflores Central Park, Huaca Pucllana archaeological site, and the vibrant nightlife of Barranco.

3. Country Club Lima Hotel

- Location: Calle Los Eucaliptos 590, San Isidro, Lima

- Price: Prices range from $280 per night for a standard room to $800 or more for luxurious suites.
- Booking Contact: +51 1 611 9000

The Country Club Lima Hotel, situated in the prestigious San Isidro district, offers a unique blend of historic charm and modern luxury. This iconic hotel is set in a beautiful 1920s mansion and is known for its classic colonial architecture and elegantly furnished rooms. Each room is decorated with antique furniture and original artwork from the Pedro de Osma Museum, offering guests a sense of Peru's rich cultural heritage.

The hotel's facilities include a serene outdoor pool, a fitness center, and a luxurious spa. Guests can enjoy gourmet dining at the hotel's award-winning restaurant, Perroquet, which is famous for its sophisticated Peruvian cuisine and exquisite seafood dishes. The hotel is adjacent to the Lima Golf Club, making it an ideal choice for golf enthusiasts. Its tranquil setting in San Isidro provides a peaceful retreat, yet it is still within a short drive from Lima's main cultural attractions and the bustling districts of Miraflores and Barranco.

Budget-Friendly Hotels

For travelers looking to explore Lima without breaking the bank, the city offers a range of comfortable and affordable accommodations. Budget-friendly hotels provide essential amenities and convenient locations, allowing visitors to enjoy the city's highlights while keeping costs down. Here are three great options for budget-conscious travelers, complete with pricing, locations, and contact information.

1. Selina Miraflores
- Location: Av. Alcanfores 425-465, Miraflores, Lima

- Price: Starting at around $20 per night for a bed in a shared dormitory, with private rooms available from $60 per night.
- Booking Contact: +51 1 642 2003

Selina Miraflores is a popular choice among backpackers and budget travelers seeking a vibrant, community-oriented atmosphere. This hostel-hotel hybrid offers a range of accommodation options, from shared dormitories to private rooms and suites. Selina's location in the heart of Miraflores makes it an ideal base for exploring Lima's best attractions, such as the Miraflores boardwalk, Kennedy Park, and local markets.

The property features a coworking space, a shared kitchen, and a bar and restaurant serving affordable meals. It also offers yoga classes, wellness activities, and events that make it easy for guests to connect with fellow travelers. Selina Miraflores is a great choice for those looking to experience Lima's lively social scene without overspending on accommodations.

2. Hotel Stefanos

- Location: Calle Esperanza 370, Miraflores, Lima
- Price: Rooms start at around $45 per night, with breakfast included.
- Booking Contact: +51 1 242 0505

Hotel Stefanos is a family-run budget hotel located in a quiet area of Miraflores, just a few blocks from Kennedy Park. The hotel offers clean, comfortable rooms with modern amenities, including free Wi-Fi, flat-screen TVs, and air conditioning. Its central location allows easy access to local restaurants, shops, and public transportation, making it convenient for exploring the city.

The hotel provides a complimentary breakfast each morning, featuring fresh fruits, bread, and traditional Peruvian dishes. The friendly staff at

Hotel Stefanos are known for their warm hospitality and are happy to assist with tour bookings and travel advice. It's a perfect option for travelers seeking a balance between affordability and convenience.

3. 1900 Backpackers Hostel

- Location: Av. Garcilaso de la Vega 1588, Centro Histórico, Lima
- Price: Shared dormitory beds start at around $10 per night, while private rooms begin at $30 per night.
- Booking Contact: +51 1 424 6909

1900 Backpackers Hostel offers a budget-friendly stay in a historic mansion located near Lima's city center. Its location provides easy access to the city's cultural sites, such as the Plaza Mayor, the San Francisco Monastery, and the Museum of the Central Reserve Bank. This hostel is ideal for travelers who want to immerse themselves in the rich history of Lima's colonial district while staying within a tight budget.

The hostel offers a range of accommodations, from basic dormitory-style beds to private rooms for couples or small groups. Facilities include a communal kitchen, a rooftop terrace with city views, and a lively bar area where guests can socialize. 1900 Backpackers Hostel also organizes walking tours of the city, providing an affordable way to discover Lima's historic attractions.

Both luxury and budget-friendly hotels in Lima offer unique experiences that cater to different types of travelers. Whether you're seeking the high-end comfort of a five-star hotel or the cozy atmosphere of a budget hostel, Lima has accommodations to suit your needs. Each option provides a gateway to exploring the city's rich cultural heritage, vibrant neighborhoods, and stunning coastal landscapes.

Chapter 9: Tourist Centers and Locations

Lima, the vibrant capital of Peru, is a city that seamlessly blends ancient history with modern life. From pre-Columbian archaeological sites to lush parks and contemporary attractions, Lima offers a wide array of must-visit spots that appeal to every type of traveler. This overview highlights some of the city's most fascinating tourist attractions, providing insight into what makes each one unique.

Overview of Must-Visit Tourist Attractions

Lima's appeal lies in its diversity of attractions. Travelers can explore the ruins of ancient civilizations, stroll through bustling parks, and encounter Peru's wildlife without ever leaving the city. Among these attractions are the archaeological site of Huaca Pucllana, the lively and central Kennedy Park, and the expansive Parque de las

Leyendas, which combines history with natural wonders. Each of these locations offers a distinct perspective on Lima's rich cultural tapestry, making them essential stops on any Lima itinerary.

Huaca Pucllana: An Ancient Wonder in the Heart of the City

- Location: General Borgoño Block 8, Miraflores, Lima
- Entry Fee: Approx. $6 (adults), $2 (students)
- Opening Hours: Tuesday to Sunday, 9:00 AM to 5:00 PM (evening tours also available)

One of Lima's most intriguing historical sites is Huaca Pucllana, a massive adobe and clay pyramid that dates back to around 400 AD. Located in the upscale district of Miraflores, this archaeological site stands as a testament to the ancient Lima culture that thrived in the region before the rise of the Inca Empire. Despite being surrounded by the urban landscape of modern Lima, Huaca Pucllana offers a glimpse into Peru's distant past.

The pyramid itself, standing at over 22 meters tall, is constructed from handmade bricks and served as an important ceremonial and administrative center. The site is divided into two main areas: one used for religious ceremonies and sacrifices, and the other as an administrative hub for political and economic activities. The presence of artifacts like pottery and textiles suggests that Huaca Pucllana was a vibrant cultural center.

A guided tour is highly recommended, as it provides valuable context about the pyramid's construction and its significance within the ancient Lima culture. Visitors can also explore a small on-site museum that houses artifacts uncovered during excavations, including pottery, textiles, and even mummified remains.

After the tour, the on-site restaurant offers a unique dining experience, where guests can enjoy traditional Peruvian dishes while overlooking the illuminated ruins. This juxtaposition of ancient history with modern comforts makes Huaca Pucllana a truly unforgettable attraction in Lima.

Kennedy Park: The Cultural Heart of Miraflores

- Location: Av. Diagonal, Miraflores, Lima
- Entry Fee: Free
- Opening Hours: Open 24 hours, with events typically occurring in the evening

Located in the center of Miraflores, **Kennedy Park** (Parque Kennedy) is one of Lima's most popular public spaces, known for its lively atmosphere, beautiful greenery, and the friendly cats that roam freely. The park serves as a social and cultural hub where both locals and tourists gather to enjoy various activities, making it an ideal spot to experience the everyday life of Lima.

The park is named after former U.S. President John F. Kennedy, reflecting Peru's historical ties with the United States. It is surrounded by cafes, restaurants, and artisanal markets, offering visitors numerous options for dining and shopping. Local artists often set up stalls around the park, selling paintings, handmade jewelry, and traditional crafts, making it a great place to pick up unique souvenirs.

In the evenings, Kennedy Park transforms into a vibrant scene with live music, dance performances, and open-air events. Local musicians and street performers entertain passersby, creating a lively ambiance that captures the spirit of Miraflores. On weekends, the park often hosts art fairs and cultural events that showcase the work of Peruvian artists and craftsmen.

One of the park's most charming features is its population of stray cats, which are lovingly cared for by local volunteers. Visitors can often spot these friendly felines lounging among the flower beds or playfully interacting with people. The cats have become an iconic part of Kennedy Park's identity, adding a touch of whimsy to this urban oasis.

For those looking to explore beyond the park, nearby attractions include the bustling streets of Av. Larco, the stunning views from the Miraflores Malecón, and the historic *Iglesia Virgen Milagrosa*, a beautiful church located at the edge of the park. Whether you're seeking a place to relax, enjoy live entertainment, or simply soak up the local atmosphere, Kennedy Park is a must-visit destination in Lima.

Parque de las Leyendas: A Journey Through Nature and History

- Location: Av. Parque de Las Leyendas 580, San Miguel, Lima
- Entry Fee: Approx. $5 (adults), $2 (children)
- Opening Hours: Monday to Sunday, 9:00 AM to 5:00 PM

Parque de las Leyendas (Park of Legends) is one of Lima's most expansive and family-friendly attractions, offering a mix of history, wildlife, and botanical wonders. Located in the San Miguel district, this park spans over 90 hectares and is home to a zoo, botanical gardens, and archaeological sites, making it a perfect destination for a full day of exploration.

One of the park's primary attractions is its zoo, which is divided into three main sections that represent the diverse ecosystems of Peru: Costa (Coast), Sierra (Highlands), and Selva (Amazon Rainforest). Each section features native animal species from these regions, providing visitors with an educational experience about Peru's rich biodiversity. Highlights include Andean condors, spectacled bears, jaguars, and various species of monkeys. The park is also home to a wide range of birds, reptiles, and marine life, making it a delight for animal lovers of all ages.

Beyond the zoo, Parque de las Leyendas is also home to several pre-Columbian ruins, including *Huaca San Miguel*, an archaeological site that dates back to the Lima culture. Visitors can explore these ancient structures, learning about the history of the people who lived in this area long before the arrival of the Spanish. The integration of historical ruins within the park's layout provides a unique opportunity to connect with Lima's ancient heritage while enjoying a day outdoors.

The park's botanical garden showcases a wide variety of plants and flowers native to Peru, creating a serene space for visitors to stroll and appreciate the natural beauty. There are also picnic areas, playgrounds, and a small lake where families can rent paddle boats. The park's facilities include restaurants and snack bars, making it easy to spend an entire day without leaving the grounds.

Parque de las Leyendas offers a unique blend of culture, history, and nature, making it a perfect spot for families, history enthusiasts, and nature lovers alike. Its convenient location in San Miguel, close to the airport, also makes it a great last stop for those looking to enjoy a bit of Lima's culture before catching a flight.

Huaca Pucllana, Kennedy Park, and Parque de las Leyendas each represent different aspects of what makes Lima a fascinating city to visit. From ancient pyramids to lively urban parks and expansive nature reserves, these attractions offer a diverse range of experiences that highlight the city's unique blend of history, culture, and natural beauty. Together, they provide a well-rounded introduction to Lima's rich heritage, making them essential destinations for any traveler looking to explore the Peruvian capital.

Chapter 10: Cultural Experiences

Lima is not just the capital of Peru but also a vibrant cultural hub that offers a rich tapestry of traditions, music, dance, and community life. Visitors to Lima will find numerous ways to connect with the city's history and people through its cultural experiences. These include opportunities to witness traditional Peruvian dances and music, partake in Lima's diverse festivals, and engage in immersive activities that promote meaningful interactions with locals. Each of these experiences provides a deeper understanding of Lima's unique cultural identity, making a trip to the city truly memorable.

Traditional Peruvian Dances and Music

One of the most enriching ways to experience Lima's culture is through its traditional dances and music, which reflect Peru's diverse heritage and regional influences. Music and dance are integral to Peruvian life, often passed down through generations as a means of storytelling, celebration, and cultural preservation.

Marinera is perhaps the most iconic of all Peruvian dances, known for its graceful movements and complex choreography. It symbolizes a romantic courtship between a man and a woman, with each dancer using a handkerchief as a prop. The dance varies slightly by region, but the *Marinera Limeña* is a distinct version native to Lima, characterized by elegant footwork and flirtatious gestures. Performances often feature live accompaniment by traditional instruments such as the guitar and cajón, a box-like percussion instrument of Afro-Peruvian origin. Visitors can watch Marinera performances at cultural centers in Lima or even take a dance class to learn the basic steps themselves.

Afro-Peruvian music and dance also play a significant role in Lima's cultural landscape. Stemming from the communities of African descent who have lived in Peru since colonial times, Afro-Peruvian traditions have significantly influenced the country's musical heritage. Dances like the *Festejo* are lively and rhythmic, featuring strong percussive elements that make them captivating to watch. The beat of the cajón, accompanied by guitars and other percussion instruments, creates a dynamic and joyful atmosphere during these performances. Various cultural centers and restaurants in Lima, such as La Candelaria in Barranco, offer visitors the chance to enjoy these captivating shows.

Another dance that holds a special place in Lima's cultural scene is the Huayno, which originates from the Andean highlands but is widely performed throughout Peru. Huayno music is characterized by its use of traditional Andean instruments like the charango (a small stringed instrument) and quena (a flute). The dance is typically performed at celebrations and social gatherings, with dancers wearing traditional attire that reflects their regional roots. Huayno's popularity in Lima demonstrates the city's role as a melting pot of cultural influences, where Andean traditions blend with coastal and urban elements.

Festivals Celebrated in Lima

Lima's festival calendar is filled with celebrations that bring the city to life, each reflecting different aspects of Peruvian identity, history, and religious devotion. These festivals are a vibrant expression of local culture and offer visitors a chance to immerse themselves in the communal spirit of Lima.

Fiestas Patrias, or Peru's Independence Day celebrations, take place on July 28th and 29th each year, commemorating the country's independence from Spanish rule. The entire city of Lima transforms during this time, with parades, concerts, and fireworks lighting up the capital. The celebrations include military parades, performances by folk dancers, and patriotic music, creating an atmosphere of national pride. Many residents display the Peruvian flag outside their homes, adding to the festive mood. Visitors to Lima during Fiestas Patrias can join in the celebrations and experience the profound sense of unity and national pride that defines this time of year.

Another significant festival is Semana Santa (Holy Week), which takes place in the week leading up to Easter. Holy Week is marked by religious processions, masses, and reenactments of biblical events, reflecting the deep-rooted Catholic faith in Peru. In Lima, the historic city center becomes the focal point of these events, with processions starting from the *Cathedral of Lima* and passing through the streets. The atmosphere is somber yet reverent, as participants carry statues of the *Virgen de la Soledad* and *El Señor de los Milagros*. Semana Santa provides a unique opportunity for visitors to observe Lima's spiritual traditions and the role of religion in everyday life.

The Feast of Señor de los Milagros, celebrated in October, is another of Lima's most significant religious events. This celebration honors an image of Christ painted by an Angolan slave in the 17th century, which has become a symbol of faith for many Peruvians. During the festival, thousands of devotees clad in purple robes participate in processions that wind through the city's streets, carrying a replica of the sacred image. The procession is accompanied by hymns, prayers, and the scent of incense, creating a deeply spiritual atmosphere. Visitors can witness the devotion and passion of Lima's residents as they express their faith, making it an emotionally moving experience.

Opportunities for Local Interactions and Learning

Beyond festivals and performances, Lima offers numerous ways for travelers to engage with local communities, learn about traditional practices, and gain a more intimate understanding of the city's way of life. Participating in these activities can create lasting memories and foster a deeper connection to the culture of Lima.

One popular way to connect with locals is through **culinary experiences**. Lima is known as the gastronomic capital of South America, and its food culture is a source of pride for Peruvians. Many local cooking classes and food tours offer visitors the chance to learn how to prepare traditional dishes like *ceviche*, *lomo saltado*, and *ají de gallina*. These experiences often include visits to local markets, where participants can learn about the variety of native ingredients that form the foundation of Peruvian cuisine. Engaging with Lima's chefs and market vendors allows travelers to gain insights into the city's culinary heritage while sharing a meal with new friends.

For those interested in Peru's indigenous heritage, craft workshops offer a hands-on way to learn about traditional arts. Workshops in activities like textile weaving, pottery making, and *jewelry crafting* are available at cultural centers in Lima and nearby artisan communities. These workshops are often led by skilled artisans who are eager to share their craft and explain the cultural significance behind their work. Visitors can take home their handmade souvenirs, which serve as a tangible reminder of their time in Lima.

Walking tours are another excellent opportunity for visitors to engage with Lima's history and local stories. Guided tours through the historic city center or the bohemian neighborhood of Barranco offer insights into Lima's colonial past, architectural heritage, and street art scene. Walking tours are often led by knowledgeable locals who provide a deeper understanding of the city's transformation over the years. These tours can be a great way to discover hidden gems, learn about Lima's social dynamics, and connect with the city on a personal level.

In addition, Lima's **community tourism initiatives** allow visitors to spend time with local families in rural areas or traditional fishing communities along the coast. These experiences often involve activities like fishing, farming, or weaving, providing a glimpse into the daily life of Peruvians outside the urban environment. Community tourism fosters cultural exchange, allowing travelers to learn directly from the people who call these places home.

Lima's rich cultural experiences, from traditional dances and music to vibrant festivals and opportunities for local interactions, offer visitors a deep and immersive way to connect with the city. Whether attending a captivating Marinera performance, celebrating during Fiestas Patrias, or learning how to cook a classic Peruvian dish, each experience provides a window into Lima's soul. By engaging with these aspects of Lima's culture, travelers can leave with a greater appreciation for the city's heritage, traditions, and the warmth of its people.

Chapter 11: Dining in Lima

Lima is celebrated as the gastronomic capital of South America, making it a premier destination for food lovers. The city's cuisine is a fusion of influences from indigenous Andean traditions, Spanish colonial history, and immigrant cultures, including African, Chinese, and Japanese. This blending of flavors has resulted in a culinary scene that is diverse, innovative, and deeply rooted in tradition. Whether you're looking for world-renowned fine dining or a casual street food experience, Lima offers a variety of restaurants that cater to all tastes and budgets. This guide highlights some of the must-visit restaurants in Lima, ranging from upscale establishments to more affordable local favorites.

Recommended Restaurants

1. Central (Fine Dining)

- Location: Av. Pedro de Osma 301, Barranco, Lima
- Cuisine: Modern Peruvian
- Reservations: Highly recommended
- Phone: +51 1 2428515

Central is one of the most acclaimed restaurants in the world and a must-visit for any food enthusiast traveling to Lima. Run by chef Virgilio Martínez, Central showcases the biodiversity of Peru by taking diners on a culinary journey through the country's various ecosystems, from the Amazon rainforest to the Andean highlands. Each dish at Central is crafted with indigenous ingredients sourced from different altitudes, reflecting Peru's rich natural heritage.

The restaurant's tasting menu features dishes that explore the depths of Peru's ingredients in creative and visually stunning ways. Expect to encounter ingredients you may have never tried before, such as *cushuro* (Andean caviar), *maca* (a Peruvian root), and *oca* (an ancient tuber). Each course is carefully designed to engage all the senses, with presentations that highlight the unique textures, colors, and flavors of Peru.

The dining experience at Central is intimate, with minimalistic décor allowing the food to be the focal point. Diners are treated to an explanation of each dish's origin and the altitude from which its ingredients are sourced, making the meal not just a culinary experience but also an educational one.

2. Maido (Fine Dining, Nikkei Cuisine)

- Location: Calle San Martin 399, Miraflores, Lima
- Cuisine: Japanese-Peruvian (Nikkei)
- Reservations: Essential
- Phone: +51 1 4462512

Maido is a world-renowned restaurant that blends Japanese and Peruvian flavors in a unique style known as Nikkei cuisine. Headed by chef Mitsuharu

Tsumura, Maido consistently ranks among the top restaurants in the world due to its innovative approach to this fusion cuisine. Peru has a significant Japanese immigrant population, and the integration of Japanese techniques with Peruvian ingredients has given rise to this celebrated culinary tradition.

At Maido, diners can enjoy a tasting menu that merges the delicate flavors of Japanese sushi and sashimi with the bold, vibrant ingredients of Peru. One of the standout dishes is the Nigiri de Paiche, a piece of Amazonian fish served sushi-style, showcasing the harmonious balance between Japanese precision and Peruvian produce. Another popular dish is tiradito, a Nikkei take on Peru's classic ceviche, blending raw fish with a light, citrus-based marinade.

Maido's atmosphere is modern yet warm, with Japanese-inspired design elements. The restaurant offers a front-row view of the open kitchen, allowing diners to watch as each dish is meticulously prepared. The attention to detail, both in flavor and presentation, ensures that every meal at Maido is a memorable experience.

3. La Mar (Seafood)

- Location: Av. La Mar 770, Miraflores, Lima
- Cuisine: Peruvian Seafood
- Reservations: No reservations; early arrival recommended
- Phone: +51 1 4213365

No trip to Lima is complete without sampling the city's renowned seafood, and **La Mar** is one of the best places to do so. This vibrant *cevichería*, located in the coastal district of Miraflores, is famous for serving fresh, high-quality seafood dishes that highlight the flavors of the Pacific Ocean. La Mar is part of a culinary empire created by Gastón Acurio, a pioneering Peruvian chef credited with putting Lima on the world's gastronomic map.

The menu at La Mar centers around ceviche, Peru's national dish, which consists of raw fish marinated in lime juice, chili peppers, and onions. One of the most popular offerings is the *Ceviche Mixto*, a dish that combines fresh fish, shrimp, squid, and octopus with a tangy leche de tigre (citrus marinade). Other standout dishes include Choritos a la Chalaca (mussels topped with a spicy salsa) and Jalea Mixta, a crispy seafood platter served with fried plantains.

The atmosphere at La Mar is casual yet lively, with an open-air dining area that captures the spirit of coastal Lima. While the restaurant doesn't take reservations, it's well worth the wait for a table, especially if you're craving some of the freshest seafood in the city.

4. Isolina (Traditional Peruvian)

- Location: Av. San Martín 101, Barranco, Lima

- Cuisine: Traditional Peruvian Creole
- Reservations: Recommended
- Phone: +51 1 2475075

Located in the bohemian district of Barranco, Isolina is a popular restaurant that offers traditional Peruvian *criollo* (Creole) dishes, which are a reflection of Lima's historical and cultural melting pot. The restaurant is known for its generous portions and home-style cooking, making it a favorite among locals and tourists alike.

Isolina's menu features hearty, flavorful dishes that are steeped in tradition. One of the restaurant's specialties is *Seco de Res*, a slow-cooked beef stew marinated in a rich cilantro sauce, served with rice and beans. Another must-try is *Chicharrón de Panceta*, crispy fried pork belly served with yucca and tangy salsa criolla. For a more adventurous palate, the restaurant offers *Cau Cau*, a traditional tripe stew that is beloved by many Peruvians.

The atmosphere at Isolina is warm and inviting, with a rustic interior that pays homage to the traditional *picanterías* (informal eateries) of Lima's past. The restaurant's relaxed vibe and focus on traditional recipes make it a great place to experience the authentic flavors of Lima's criollo cuisine.

5. Panchita (Traditional Peruvian)

- Location: Calle 2 de Mayo 298, Miraflores, Lima
- Cuisine: Traditional Peruvian
- Reservations: Recommended
- Phone: +51 1 2425957

Panchita is another gem in Lima's culinary scene, offering a wide range of traditional Peruvian dishes with a focus on the country's coastal and Andean flavors. Part of Gastón Acurio's restaurant group, Panchita specializes in *anticuchos* (grilled skewers), a popular street food that dates back to pre-Columbian times. The most famous dish is the *Anticucho de Corazón*, made from marinated beef heart grilled to perfection, which has become a beloved delicacy in Lima.

The menu at Panchita also includes other classic Peruvian dishes like *Ají de Gallina* (a creamy chicken stew) and *Lomo Saltado* (stir-fried beef with onions, tomatoes, and fries). For dessert, the *Picarones* (sweet, fried doughnuts made from squash and sweet potato) are a must-try.

With its lively atmosphere and rustic décor, Panchita provides a welcoming space for visitors to enjoy traditional Peruvian flavors in a casual setting. The restaurant's emphasis on quality ingredients and time-honored recipes ensures that diners leave with a full stomach and a greater appreciation for Peru's rich culinary heritage.

6. El Mercado (Seafood)

- Location: Hipólito Unanue 203, Miraflores, Lima
- Cuisine: Peruvian Seafood
- Reservations: Recommended
- Phone: +51 1 2211322

El Mercado is another top destination for seafood lovers, offering a relaxed yet stylish dining experience. This restaurant, owned by chef Rafael Osterling, focuses on fresh, seasonal ingredients, ensuring that every dish showcases the best of what the ocean has to offer.

One of the standout dishes at El Mercado is the *Ceviche Clásico*, a fresh, zesty dish that highlights the simplicity and boldness of Peruvian flavors. Other popular items include *Pulpo al Olivo* (octopus with olive sauce) and *Tiradito Nikkei*, a Japanese-Peruvian fusion dish that combines raw fish with a tangy soy-based sauce.

The atmosphere at El Mercado is casual and vibrant, with an open-air dining area that captures the energy of a bustling market. The restaurant's emphasis on sustainability and local sourcing makes it a great choice for eco-conscious diners looking to enjoy Lima's seafood offerings.

Lima's dining scene is a true reflection of the city's cultural diversity and culinary innovation. From the fine-dining experiences at Central and Maido to the traditional flavors at Isolina and Panchita, there's no shortage of options for food lovers in the Peruvian capital. Whether you're indulging in fresh ceviche or savoring hearty criollo dishes, dining in Lima is sure to be one of the highlights of any trip. Each restaurant offers a unique way to experience Peru's rich culinary heritage, ensuring

Made in the USA
Middletown, DE
14 January 2025

69457118R00066